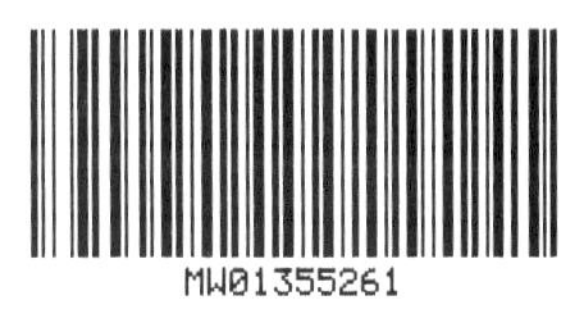

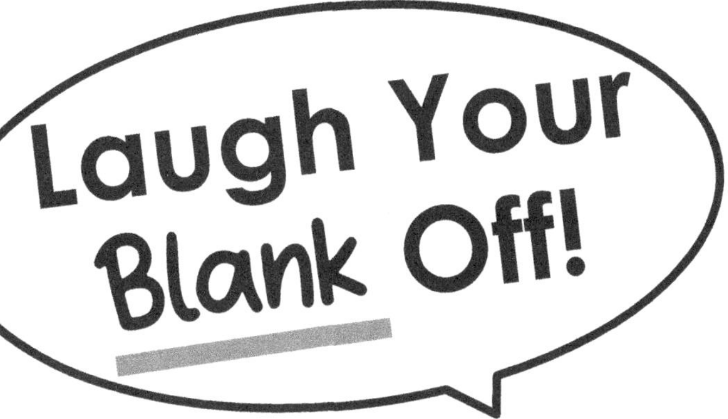

Ad Libs for Adults 😂

Halloween Edition

JBC Story Press

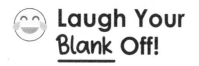

Welcome! And get ready to *Laugh Your Blank Off!*

Number of players: 2-200+

There's really no limit... The more the merrier! This game is perfect for parties or just hanging out with friends. Players don't even have to be in the same room. Playing through video chat works great too.

Inside, you'll find 21 entertaining stories with blank spaces where words have been left out. Each story comes with a list of missing words of various types, e.g., ADJECTIVE, ADVERB, NOUN, EXCLAMATION, etc.

For each story, one player is the Story Teller. The Story Teller asks the other players to call out words to fill in the spaces of the story — WITHOUT first telling them what the story is about.

And bam! Just like that, you have a RIDICULOUSLY funny story!

The Story Teller reads the completed story out loud, and you all laugh so hard you almost pee your pants, cry, roll on the floor, or all of the above! *YOU* fill in the blank!

Adult Themes

This version of the game is for "grownups." That means stories may contain references to alcohol, romance, and other crazy adult stuff (you know, like work or parenting). Whether stories include "adult" language is up to you! Some groups like to use "spicy" swear words. Others prefer "sweet" and swear-free. It's your call!

One thing's for sure. Every story you create will be RIDICULOUSLY funny!

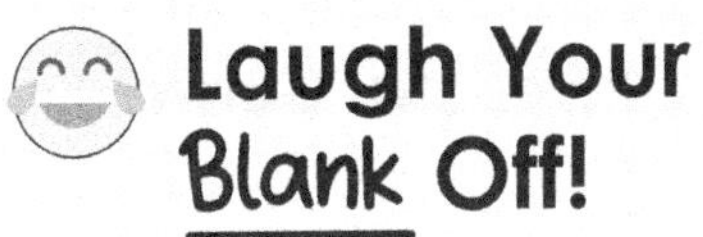

Ad Libs for Adults
How to Play

Examples

Before, with blanks:

"____________ (EXCLAMATION)! We need to ____________ (VERB) to the party as ____________ (ADVERB ENDING IN "LY") as possible. We only have ______ (NUMBER) minutes to get there." So we jumped in the ____________ (ADJECTIVE) car and sped off.

After the Story Teller fills in the blanks with words from the players

"____Yuck____ (EXCLAMATION)! We need to ____dance____ (VERB) to the party as ____quietly____ (ADVERB ENDING IN "LY") as possible. We only have __900__ (NUMBER) minutes to get there." So we jumped in the ___furry____ (ADJECTIVE) car and sped off.

Quick Review

ADJECTIVE – Describes something or someone. Examples: Funny, huge, bossy, lame, fast.

ADVERB – Describes how something is done. You will only be asked for adverbs that end in "ly". Examples: Happily, badly, loudly.

NOUN or PLURAL NOUN – A person, place or thing. Examples: Singular – sister, book, foot. Plural – sisters, books, feet.

VERB, VERB ENDING IN "ING" or VERB (PAST TENSE) – Verbs are action words. Examples: Verb – Run, kiss, sing; Verb ending in "ing"– running, kissing, singing; Verb (past tense) – ran, kissed, sang

EXCLAMATION – A sound, word, or phrase that is spoken suddenly or loudly and expresses emotions, like excitement or anger, or shock or pain. Examples: "Oh no!", "Awesome!", "You're kidding me!", "Oof!"

OTHER – Specific words, like ANIMAL, BODY PART, CITY, COLOR, FIRST NAME (FRIEND)

NOUN
ADJECTIVE
ADJECTIVE
CELEBRITY NAME
ADJECTIVE
VERB
CLOTHING ITEM (PLURAL)
FIRST NAME (ANYONE)
NOUN
NUMBER
PLURAL NOUN
ADJECTIVE
VERB
VERB
ADVERB ENDING IN "LY"
COLOR
ADJECTIVE
PLURAL NOUN
VERB

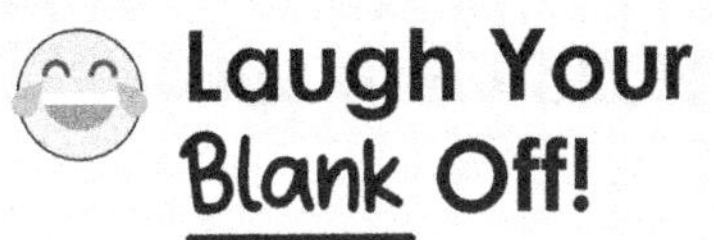

Five-Star Scare

The reviews are in! It's safe to say that *Night of* ____________ (NOUN) is the ____________ (ADJECTIVE) Halloween movie to hit theaters in years. Whether it's the ____________ (ADJECTIVE) performance of the star-studded cast, including ____________ (CELEBRITY NAME), or the ____________ (ADJECTIVE) effects, this film is sure to ____________ (VERB) your ____________ (CLOTHING ITEM (PLURAL)) off. Director ____________ (FIRST NAME (ANYONE)) Mc____________ (NOUN) took the movie in a perfect direction, staying true to the spirit of the original horror film that premiered ______ (NUMBER) years ago. But, the modern twist is sure to keep audiences glued to their ____________ (PLURAL NOUN). The story plot starts off a little ____________ (ADJECTIVE), but the characters keep you interested. As soon as that first ____________ (VERB) scare hits, however, the plot takes a turn you could never predict. The suspense builds as characters mysteriously ____________ (VERB), and the gore is ____________ (ADVERB ENDING IN "LY") realistic. So much ____________ (COLOR) blood runs through the streets of the ____________ (ADJECTIVE) town, that even the most seasoned horror ____________ (PLURAL NOUN) are bound to freak out. So, what are you waiting for? ____________ (VERB) to your local movie theater now!"

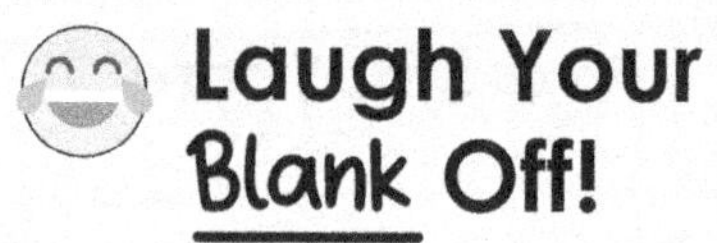

Halloween Spirits

VERB ENDING IN "ING"
ADJECTIVE
VERB
FIRST NAME (ANYONE)
FRUIT
FOOD
COLOR
VEGETABLE
ADJECTIVE
EMOTION
VERB ENDING IN "ING"
ANIMAL (PLURAL)
VERB
CITY
FOOD
FOOD
NOUN

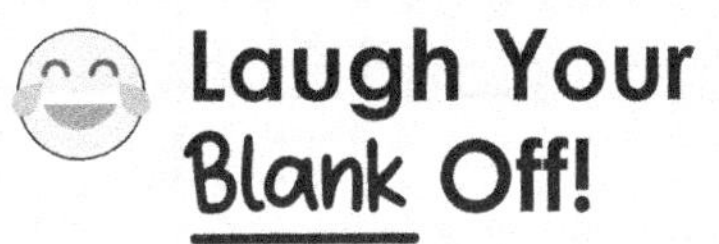

Halloween Spirits

Calling all party ghosts! Oops, make that party *hosts*! Do you need a sure-fire way to send Halloween spirits ____________ (VERB ENDING IN "ING")? We've got you covered with ____________ (ADJECTIVE) cocktail ideas that will ____________ (VERB) all your ghoul friends *and* guy friends! First, a classic Bloody ____________ (FIRST NAME (ANYONE)) can be served any time of the day or night. Or, make some poison ____________ (FRUIT) cocktails to sip with your favorite witches. For something scarier, try Death-by-____________ (FOOD) spiked milkshakes or slime ____________ (COLOR) Jello shots. And no Halloween party is complete without Candy ____________ (VEGETABLE)! Garnish your cocktails with it or whip it into ____________ (ADJECTIVE) daiquiris. ____________ (EMOTION) about guests sugar crashing? Caffeine to the rescue! Pumpkin Espresso Martinis will keep your guests ____________ (VERB ENDING IN "ING") through the night. Of course, your spooky friends will be as hungry as ____________ (ANIMAL (PLURAL)) after dancing the Monster ____________ (VERB), so be sure to serve killer snacks too. ____________ (CITY)-style Batwings, Deviled ____________ (FOOD) and Mummy Wraps are awfully good! And for dessert, lots of ____________ (FOOD) of course! If you don't want to get stuck with too much leftover candy, fill some ____________ (NOUN) bags for all your guests.

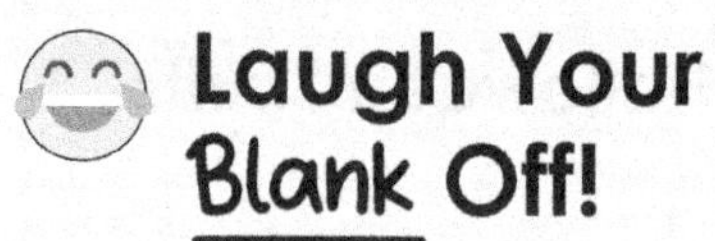

Crazy Candy Corn Lady

FIRST NAME (ANYONE)
ADJECTIVE
ANIMAL (PLURAL)
FIRST NAME (FRIEND)
NUMBER
ADJECTIVE
BODY PART
ADJECTIVE
VERB ENDING IN “ING”
NUMBER
ADJECTIVE
NOUN
EXCLAMATION
ADVERB ENDING IN “LY”
VERB
VERB
NOUN
NOUN

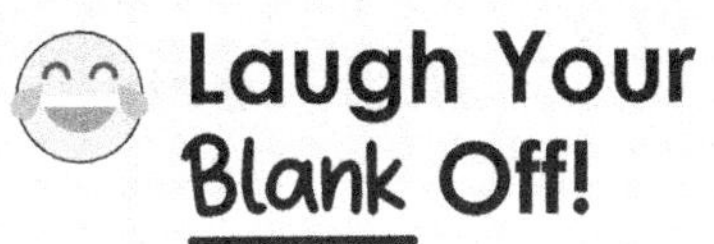

Crazy Candy Corn Lady

You have probably heard the stories about ____________ the
FIRST NAME (ANYONE)

____________ Ghost, Count Dracula, and people who turn into
ADJECTIVE

____________ when the moon is full. But have you heard the
ANIMAL (PLURAL)

story about the Crazy Candy Corn Lady? This Lady is named

____________ and she is an old friend of mine. When we were
FIRST NAME (FRIEND)

just ______ years-old, her obsession began. It was a fateful
NUMBER

October evening when she received her first bag of

____________ candy corn. She slowly lifted a piece to her
ADJECTIVE

____________ and took a bite. From that moment on, she was
BODY PART

never the same. Every day she ate more and more of these

____________ treats. Soon she was ____________ up to
ADJECTIVE VERB ENDING IN "ING"

____________ pieces a day. She was completely ____________.
NUMBER ADJECTIVE

After Halloween was over, and the striped sweets disappeared

from ____________ shelves, she would go nuts. "____________!"
NOUN EXCLAMATION

she would scream. WHERE IS MY CANDY CORN?! She

searched ____________ for more candy corn. When she couldn't
ADVERB ENDING IN "LY"

____________ any, she just got crazier. Nowadays, I rarely
VERB

____________ her during October. She spends all her
VERB

____________ buying as much candy corn as possible, so she
NOUN

can feed her ____________ year around.
NOUN

High-Tech Trick-or-Treat

VERB
NOUN
NOUN
VERB ENDING IN “ING”
ADJECTIVE
CITY
EXCLAMATION
ADJECTIVE
NOUN
VEGETABLE
NOUN
VERB ENDING IN “ING”
VERB
PLURAL NOUN
ADJECTIVE
NOUN
NUMBER
ADJECTIVE
EMOTION

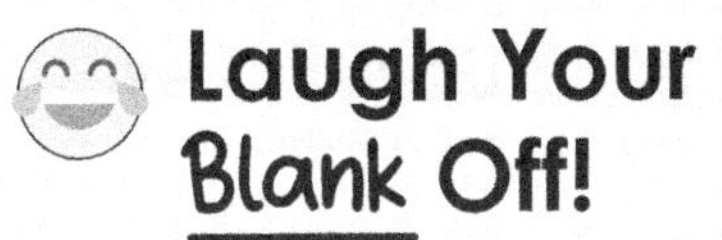

High-Tech Trick-or-Treat

Have you heard about the latest technology craze? Trick-or-treaters can now ____________ (VERB) out their candy collection route using an app called Maximum Treat Technology. This Halloween, the chances are good that every spooky ____________ (NOUN) and silly ____________ (NOUN) you see will be using it. Kids are not the only ones ____________ (VERB ENDING IN "ING") this ____________ (ADJECTIVE) app. Parents across ____________ (CITY) are raving about it. "____________ (EXCLAMATION)!" said one parent. "This app is ____________ (ADJECTIVE)!" Parents love that their children can share their exact ____________ (NOUN) so they never get lost in the neighborhood or local ____________ (VEGETABLE) maze during Halloween adventures. On the app, kids appear as glowing ____________ (NOUN) icons ____________ (VERB ENDING IN "ING") across the map. "It's kind of like watching a game of PAC-MAN," one parent said. "The kids ____________ (VERB) as many treats as they can while their parents chase them." And kids love sharing ____________ (PLURAL NOUN) with their friends, so everyone knows which houses are giving out the best and the ____________ (ADJECTIVE) treats. If a house is giving out full-sized ____________ (NOUN) bars, they will probably get ______ (NUMBER) stars. And the ones who hand out ____________ (ADJECTIVE) stuff, like pencils? They better brace themselves for a lot of ____________ (EMOTION) emojis.

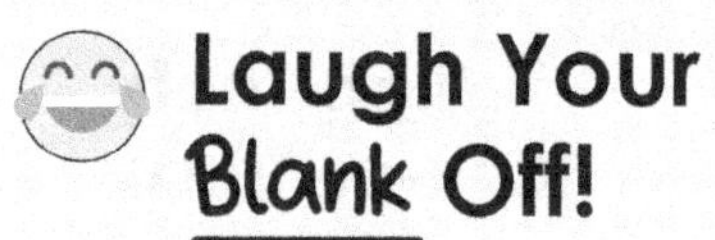

Drink Up Witches

ADJECTIVE
ADJECTIVE
ADJECTIVE
ADJECTIVE
OCCUPATION
FIRST NAME (FRIEND 1)
PLURAL NOUN
EXCLAMATION
NOUN
VERB
VERB ENDING IN “ING”
NOUN
VERB ENDING IN “ING”
FIRST NAME (FRIEND 2)
ADJECTIVE
NOUN
EXCLAMATION
FOOD
VERB (PAST TENSE)

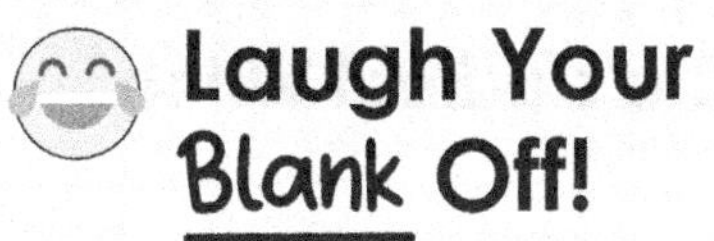

Drink Up Witches

It had been way too long since my friends and I had enjoyed a

Girls' Night Out. So, we decided to make the night extra

____________ by going out on Halloween. We were so
ADJECTIVE

____________ to get together again! We all agreed to wear
ADJECTIVE

____________ costumes, and I dressed up as a ____________
ADJECTIVE ADJECTIVE

____________. When I got to my friend ____________'s house,
OCCUPATION FIRST NAME (FRIEND 1)

we all screamed and hugged and had a few ____________.
PLURAL NOUN

"____________!" I said, looking at my ____________, "We should
EXCLAMATION NOUN

____________." We went to our favorite bar, The ____________
VERB VERB ENDING IN "ING"

____________. As soon as we got there, we started
NOUN

____________. The rest of the night was kind of a blur. But, I do
VERB ENDING IN "ING"

remember ____________ winning a prize for her ____________
FIRST NAME (FRIEND 2) ADJECTIVE

____________ costume. "____________!" we cheered, when she
NOUN EXCLAMATION

went up on stage to get her trophy. The evening ended with us

getting late-night ____________ before heading home. But not
FOOD

until we had ____________ each other we wouldn't wait so long
VERB (PAST TENSE)

to have our next Girls' Night Out!

She's a Real Witch

FIRST NAME (FRIEND)
ADJECTIVE
ANIMAL
NUMBER
COLOR
ANIMAL
MODE OF TRANSPORTATION
NOUN
VERB
NOUN
PLURAL NOUN
SILLY SOUND
VERB
CLOTHING ITEM (PLURAL)
CLOTHING ITEM (PLURAL)
EXCLAMATION

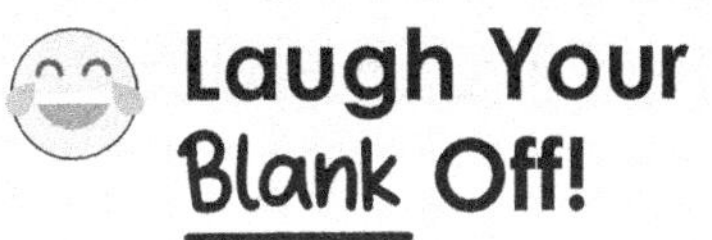

She's a Real Witch

I hate to say it, but lately, our friend, ____________ (FIRST NAME (FRIEND)), has been acting like a real *witch*. It's like a(n) ____________ (ADJECTIVE) spell has come over her. First, she used to be a(n) ____________ (ANIMAL) person. She owned ______ (NUMBER) of them and did everything for them. Then, one day, out of the ____________ (COLOR), she gave all of them to her sister and got herself a new pet: a black ____________ (ANIMAL). Her next suspicious move was to change the way she gets to work. She used to ride the ____________ (MODE OF TRANSPORTATION). Now, she rides an electric ____________ (NOUN)! It's kind of nice for her, actually, because at home it also ____________ (VERB) her floors clean. To make things worse, she now has a new ____________ (NOUN) — a really weird cackle. I used to love it when she laughed at my ____________ (PLURAL NOUN). Not anymore! Not when I hear her make that "____________ (SILLY SOUND)!" sound. Her wardrobe has also changed dramatically. And I do mean dramatically! She used to ____________ (VERB) bright colors. Now she only wears black, from head to toe. And speaking of her head and toes. You won't believe the pointy ____________ (CLOTHING ITEM (PLURAL)) and ____________ (CLOTHING ITEM (PLURAL)) she wears on her head and feet. Talk about what *not* to wear. ____________ (EXCLAMATION)!

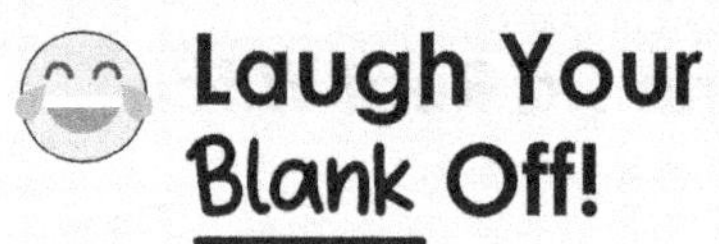

The Halloween Police

VERB
ADJECTIVE
PLURAL NOUN
NOUN
NOUN
PLURAL NOUN
PLURAL NOUN
NUMBER
NOUN
NOUN
PLURAL NOUN
VERB ENDING IN “ING”
ANIMAL (PLURAL)
VERB (PAST TENSE)
ADJECTIVE

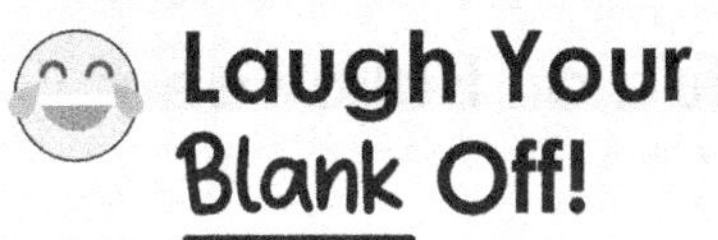

The Halloween Police

Dear Shady Acres Residents — In light of recent events, we have new rules for trick-or-treating this year. They are non-negotiable. If you do not ____________ (VERB) these ____________ (ADJECTIVE) rules, there will be consequences. Please, look at the list below and tell your ____________ (PLURAL NOUN). 1) You MUST put your ____________ (NOUN) light on to signal that you are handing out ____________ (NOUN). 2) No costumes with weapons, such as sharp ____________ (PLURAL NOUN) or chainsaws. 3) ____________ (PLURAL NOUN) must be worn at all times, by all trick-or-treaters, for their safety. 4) Cars should drive ______ (NUMBER) mph or below during trick-or-treating hours. 5) Residents may not give out candy with these allergens: ____________ (NOUN), ____________ (NOUN), or tree nuts. 6) Pranks will not be tolerated. If we see anyone with toilet paper, ____________ (PLURAL NOUN), or eggs for ____________ (VERB ENDING IN "ING") at houses, they will be taken into custody. 7) Pet ____________ (ANIMAL (PLURAL)) must remain on leash. 8) All candy must be brought to the inspection station for approval. Candy that fails inspection will be ____________ (VERB (PAST TENSE)). These rules are NON-NEGOTIABLE. If you do not follow them, you will be fined and confined to your house. Thank you for your ____________ (ADJECTIVE) cooperation.

The Shady Acres Home Owners Association

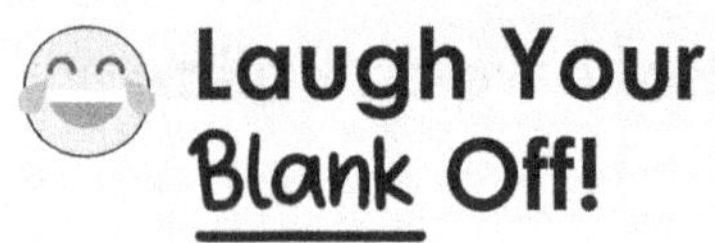

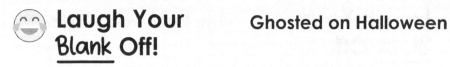

Ghosted on Halloween

ADJECTIVE
NOUN
ADJECTIVE
ADJECTIVE
EXCLAMATION
OCCUPATION
FRUIT
ADJECTIVE
VERB
ADJECTIVE
COLOR
ADJECTIVE
ADJECTIVE
VERB ENDING IN “ING”
ROOM IN HOUSE
PLURAL NOUN
EMOTION

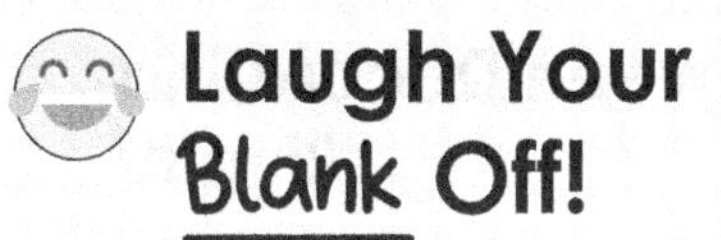

Ghosted on Halloween

I went to a(n) ____________ Halloween party this weekend, and
ADJECTIVE
the strangest thing happened. The night started out normally
enough: I put on my ____________ costume and went to my
NOUN
friend's house. When I got to the party, there were tables loaded
with ____________ food and ____________ beverages.
ADJECTIVE ADJECTIVE
"____________!" I yelped, when a skeleton spoke to me.
EXCLAMATION
Fortunately, it was just the ____________ offering me a drink
OCCUPATION
served in a small hollowed out ____________. It was
FRUIT
____________! Then I hit the ____________ floor with some
ADJECTIVE VERB
friends. When they left to get refills, a(n) ____________ guy came
ADJECTIVE
up to me. He was dressed up as, ____________-beard, the
COLOR
famous pirate. We instantly clicked. I don't know if it was his
____________ sense of humor or his ____________ eyes that
ADJECTIVE ADJECTIVE
attracted me most, but we spent the rest of the night
____________ and laughing. As the party was winding down, I
VERB ENDING IN "ING"
excused myself to go to the ____________. I was pretty sure we'd
ROOM IN HOUSE
be exchanging ____________ when I got back. But then I couldn't
PLURAL NOUN
find him anywhere! I was completely ____________, so I asked
EMOTION
my friend if he had the pirate's number. But he said that there
hadn't been a single pirate at the party all night. What if I was
ghosted by a *real* ghost?!

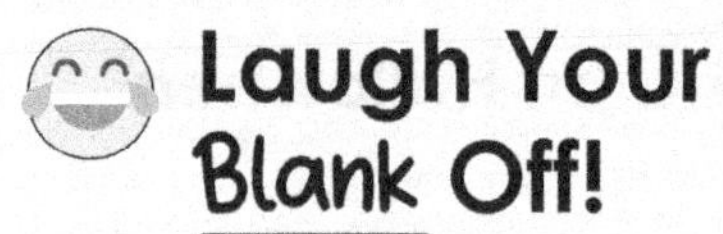

Halloween Decorating Rivalry

FIRST AND LAST NAME (FRIEND)
CITY
ADJECTIVE
NUMBER
FIRST NAME (ANYONE)
NOUN
NUMBER
NUMBER
FIRST NAME (ANYONE)
NOUN
EMOTION
COLOR
ADJECTIVE
ADJECTIVE
PLURAL NOUN
ADJECTIVE
BODY PART
VERB
ADJECTIVE

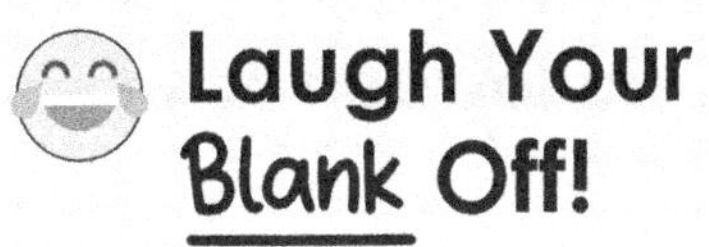

Halloween Decorating Rivalry

This is ____________, reporting for YNN, with some lighter news.
FIRST AND LAST NAME (FRIEND)

Every year, two long-time neighbors in ____________ try to outdo
CITY

each other with ____________ Halloween decorations. Sources
ADJECTIVE

tell me that this ______-year rivalry started when ____________
NUMBER FIRST NAME (ANYONE)

Mc____________ put ______ skeletons and ______ tombstones
NOUN NUMBER NUMBER

in his yard. For fun, he put the name of his neighbor,

____________ ____________-smith on one of the tombstones.
FIRST NAME (ANYONE) NOUN

His neighbor did *not* laugh at his joke however. “I was very

____________, so I showed him.” To retaliate, he set up
EMOTION

____________ strobe lights and pointed them at his neighbor’s
COLOR

windows. Every year, sources tell me, these ____________
ADJECTIVE

neighbors try to best each other with more decorations, including

____________ inflatables, spooky ____________ that play all
ADJECTIVE PLURAL NOUN

night, ____________ monsters and more. Asked if this rivalry has
ADJECTIVE

gotten a little out of ____________, some kids said they
BODY PART

____________ it because, “those ____________ guys also
VERB ADJECTIVE

compete to give out the most candy!”

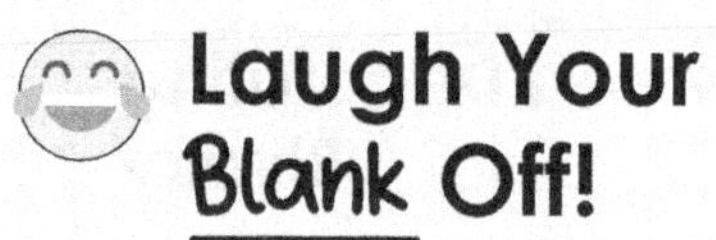

Halloween Bash

NOUN
BODY PART
PLURAL NOUN
ALCOHOLIC SPIRIT
NOUN
VERB
BODY PART (PLURAL)
BODY PART
ADJECTIVE
SPORT
CITY
ADJECTIVE
VERB
NOUN
NOUN
NOUN

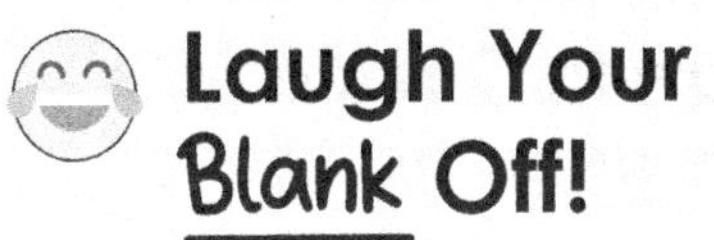

Halloween Bash

Calling all “grownup” ghouls and goblins! This Halloween is the Grand Opening of Club ____________ NOUN ! From the front door to the dance floor, you’ll be screaming your ____________ BODY PART off! With excitement, of course! The bouncers will be dressed as ____________ PLURAL NOUN, but never fear. Admission is free for everyone wearing a costume. When you enter, you’ll be offered a free shot of ____________ ALCOHOLIC SPIRIT. Just a little liquid ____________ NOUN to get you through the Club’s haunted maze of zombies, vampires and werewolves… oh my! If you ____________ VERB easily, stay close to your friends and hold ____________ BODY PART (PLURAL). Our “boo-tenders” have created chilling cocktails for you to enjoy: “The Exorcist Martini” will make your ____________ BODY PART spin; “The Psycho Mojito” will drive you ____________ ADJECTIVE, and the “Friday the 13th Cosmo” is served by a guy wearing a ____________ SPORT mask. ____________ CITY’s most famous DJ will play all your ____________ ADJECTIVE tracks, including classics like *Thriller* and the *Monster* ____________ VERB. So dress up like a ____________ NOUN or a ____________ NOUN and come to the Club! Best costume will win the Grand Prize — an all-expenses paid luxury ____________ NOUN to Transylvania!

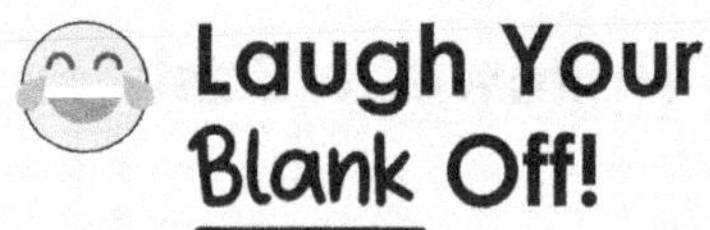

How to Get Rid of a Halloween Hangover

ADJECTIVE
ADJECTIVE
VERB ENDING IN "ING"
NOUN
ADJECTIVE
ADJECTIVE
VERB
LIQUID
NOUN
ADJECTIVE
ANIMAL
VERB
FOOD
NUMBER
VERB
NOUN
ADJECTIVE
ADJECTIVE

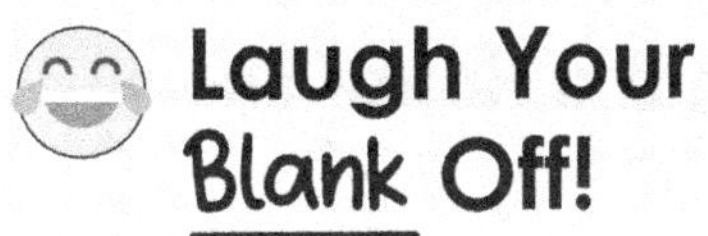

How to Get Rid of a Halloween Hangover

Halloween is one of the ____________ (ADJECTIVE) nights of the year for partying with friends. It's a time for ____________ (ADJECTIVE) costumes, ____________ (VERB ENDING IN "ING"), and eating ____________ (NOUN). Beware though friends! If you overdo the fun, you can end up with a(n) ____________ (ADJECTIVE) hangover that lasts for hours! That's why we've put together a(n) ____________ (ADJECTIVE) list of cures to help you ____________ (VERB) a Halloween hangover. 1) Drink plenty of ____________ (LIQUID) throughout the night. This is not a cure so much as a preventative ____________ (NOUN). If you stay hydrated, you should feel pretty ____________ (ADJECTIVE) in the morning.

2) Hair of the ____________ (ANIMAL). Your doctor probably wouldn't ____________ (VERB) this, but many people swear it is a sure-fire way to get rid of your hangover. Just don't go overboard! 3) Carb up! Whether you order greasy ____________ (FOOD) or whip up some pancakes in the morning, getting carbs into your system will make you feel like ________ (NUMBER) bucks. 4) ____________ (VERB) some leftover Halloween candy. Alcohol can cause low blood-sugar. A dose of ____________ (NOUN) might be just the medicine you need. 5) Sleep it off. A(n) ____________ (ADJECTIVE) nap is the ultimate hangover remedy. With a little candy in your system, you're bound to have ____________ (ADJECTIVE) dreams!

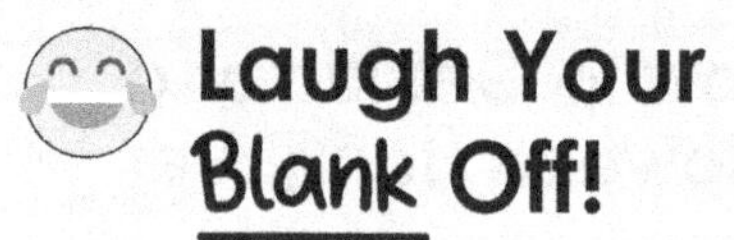

What a Horror Show

VERB
ADJECTIVE
ADJECTIVE
PLURAL NOUN
ADJECTIVE
COLOR
ALCOHOLIC SPIRIT
FIRST NAME (ANYONE)
EXCLAMATION
CLOTHING ITEM (PLURAL)
LIQUID
ADJECTIVE
EMOTION
VERB ENDING IN "ING"
NOUN
VERB ENDING IN "ING"

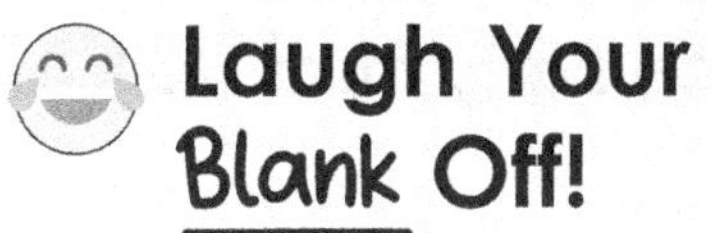

What a Horror Show

Don't get me wrong, I _____________ (VERB) Halloween. But our annual Halloween party got so _____________ (ADJECTIVE) last year, I don't think I can do it again! My husband and I dressed as _____________ (ADJECTIVE) _____________ (PLURAL NOUN). All our friends came and we were having a blast. My husband made his famous _____________ (ADJECTIVE) _____________ (COLOR) punch. But I think he must have poured in way too much _____________ (ALCOHOLIC SPIRIT). Because as soon as people started drinking it, the night took a crazy turn. Our friend who came as _____________ (FIRST NAME (ANYONE))-enstein started shouting "_____________ (EXCLAMATION)!" over and over again. Our mummy friends completely unraveled, revealing that they weren't wearing any _____________ (CLOTHING ITEM (PLURAL)) under their costumes. Our Dracula friends chased other guests around saying "I want to drink your _____________ (LIQUID)." And our witch friends turned into _____________ (ADJECTIVE) clean freaks, sweeping every room in the house. I was actually _____________ (EMOTION) when the cops showed up. I thought they were there to restore the peace. But instead of _____________ (VERB ENDING IN "ING") the party, they helped themselves to some punch. They weren't real police after all! We tried to send guests home at that point, but most of them slept on our _____________ (NOUN). The next day was like a scene from the _____________ (VERB ENDING IN "ING") Dead. Scary!

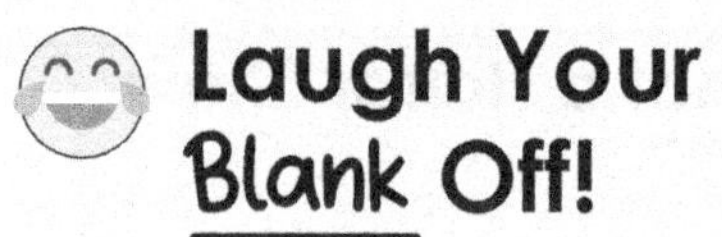

Office Party from Hell

EXCLAMATION
NOUN
VERB (PAST TENSE)
NOUN
VERB
PLURAL NOUN
NOUN
ADJECTIVE
PLURAL NOUN
NOUN
ADJECTIVE
ADJECTIVE
BODY PART
ADJECTIVE
COLOR
PLURAL NOUN
ADJECTIVE
ADJECTIVE
NOUN
BODY PART

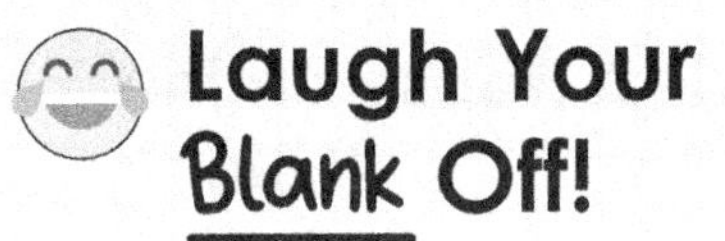

Office Party from Hell

Halloween fell on a Monday this year. Mondays are always scary, but at the last minute this year, my boss decided to throw a party

at the office. "____________!" she said. "No one's getting any
EXCLAMATION

____________ done anyway." So everyone ____________ into
NOUN VERB (PAST TENSE)

action. The Director of ____________ volunteered to
NOUN

____________ food and drinks. The Head of Human
VERB

____________ started making decorations out of ____________
PLURAL NOUN NOUN

supplies. And everyone scrambled to make ____________
ADJECTIVE

costumes from ____________ around the office. We had so many
PLURAL NOUN

mummies wrapped in ____________ paper from the restrooms,
NOUN

that we almost ran out! Tech Support played ____________
ADJECTIVE

music and ____________ sounds that made my ____________
ADJECTIVE BODY PART

crawl. They also flooded the office with ____________
ADJECTIVE

____________ lights. Someone piled horrifying ____________ of
COLOR PLURAL NOUN

paperwork on our desks. But the scariest surprise came from our

boss. She thought it would be ____________ to hand out
ADJECTIVE

____________ performance reports during the party. We got her
ADJECTIVE

back, though, by posting a photo of her dancing on a

____________ to the company's ____________-book page.
NOUN BODY PART

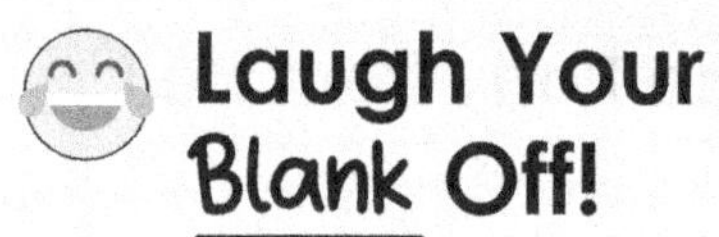

Scariest House on the Block

ADJECTIVE	
BODY PART	
ADJECTIVE	
PLURAL NOUN	
NOUN	
PLURAL NOUN	
NOUN	
COLOR	
NUMBER	
ADJECTIVE	
YEAR	
PLURAL NOUN	
NOUN	
NUMBER	
COLOR	
VERB ENDING IN "ING"	
EMOTION	
ADJECTIVE	

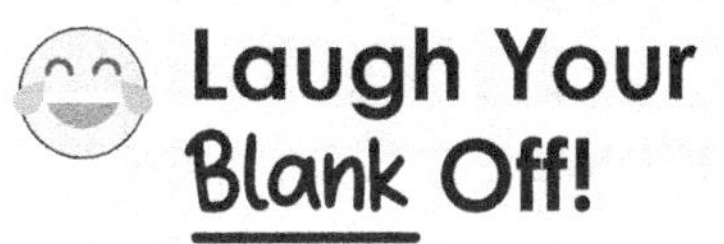

Scariest House on the Block

It seems like every neighborhood has one. That one mysterious house that everyone avoids. In our neighborhood, there's a house that is so ____________ (ADJECTIVE), it makes the hair on my ____________ (BODY PART) stick up. Next to the other houses on the block, it looks pretty ____________ (ADJECTIVE). But I hear plenty of ____________ (PLURAL NOUN) about the inhabitants. Some say there is an evil ____________ (NOUN) living there that eats ____________ (PLURAL NOUN) for dinner. Others say a ____________ (NOUN) haunts it, and no one truly lives there. The house is dark ____________ (COLOR) and has ________ (NUMBER) floors. The architecture looks old and ____________ (ADJECTIVE), like it was built in ____________ (YEAR), but no one knows for sure. Even if kids were brave enough to ring the bell on Halloween, the yard is so overgrown with thick ____________ (PLURAL NOUN), that they would need a sharp ____________ (NOUN) to cut a path to the door. My friend said she once saw a witch outside the house as she rode by on her bike. The witch was ______ (NUMBER) feet tall with ____________ (COLOR) skin. My friend was so startled, she lost her balance and fell. The next thing she knew, the witch was ____________ (VERB ENDING IN "ING") over her with a(n) ____________ (EMOTION) look on her face. My friend ran away as fast as she could! Whether these rumors are ____________ (ADJECTIVE) or not, doesn't matter. I won't be walking by that house any time soon!

Freakin' Easy Halloween Cookies

ADJECTIVE
VERB ENDING IN "ING"
ADJECTIVE
COLOR
NOUN
NUMBER
FLAVOR
NOUN
COLOR
COLOR
PLURAL NOUN
ADJECTIVE
NUMBER
VERB
ADJECTIVE
ADVERB ENDING IN "LY"
NUMBER
COLOR
VERB

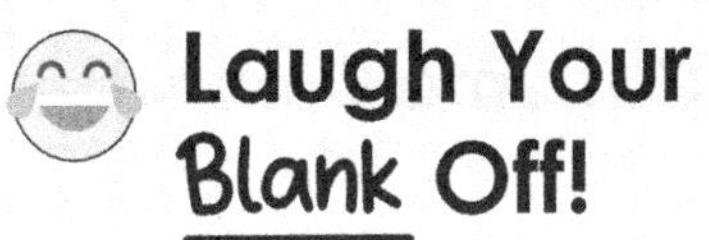

Freakin' Easy Halloween Cookies

With Halloween just around the corner, we're sharing a(n)

____________ recipe that will have your kids ____________ like
ADJECTIVE VERB ENDING IN "ING"

werewolves with pleasure.

You'll need these ingredients:

1 cup ____________ butter
ADJECTIVE

¾ cup of ____________ sugar
COLOR

1 ____________ vanilla
NOUN

____________ egg(s)
NUMBER

1 ____________ pudding mix
FLAVOR

½ teaspoon of baking ____________
NOUN

1/2 cup ____________ and ____________ sprinkles
COLOR COLOR

¾ cup chocolate ____________. Then follow these
PLURAL NOUN

____________ steps: 1) Preheat your oven to ______ degrees. 2)
ADJECTIVE NUMBER

____________ butter, sugar, and eggs. 3) Add the vanilla,
VERB

chocolate, and pudding mix and stir until ____________. 4) Mix in
ADJECTIVE

the rest of the ingredients until ____________ combined. 5) Place
ADVERB ENDING IN "LY"

the cookie dough balls on a baking sheet and bake for ______
NUMBER

minutes until golden ____________. 6) Add sprinkles to the
COLOR

cookies and let cool until you can ____________ them to your
VERB

werewolves!

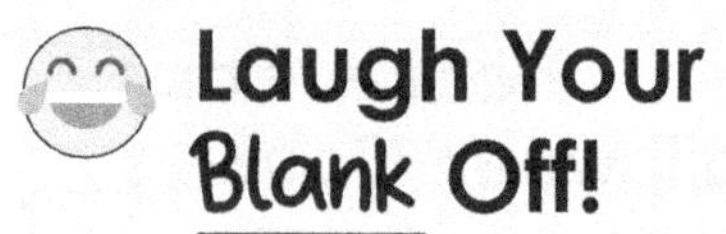

Adult Costume Contest

EXCLAMATION
ADJECTIVE
ADJECTIVE
EMOTION
FIRST NAME (FRIEND 1)
FIRST NAME (FRIEND 2)
ADJECTIVE
BIRD
FOOD
VERB
BODY PART
ADJECTIVE
PLURAL NOUN
ADJECTIVE
ADJECTIVE
OCCUPATION
ADJECTIVE
ADJECTIVE
SPORT
NUMBER

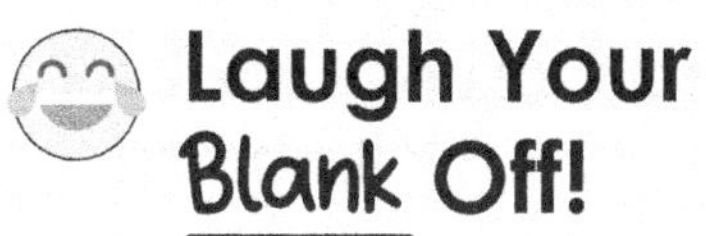

Adult Costume Contest

Attention everyone! The final votes of our costume contest are in.

____________! We had so many ____________ entries! But only
EXCLAMATION ADJECTIVE

a lucky few will win these ____________ prizes. First up, is the
ADJECTIVE

Best Couples Costumes category. I am ____________ to
EMOTION

announce that our winners are ____________ and
FIRST NAME (FRIEND 1)

____________, disguised as a(n) ____________ pirate and their
FIRST NAME (FRIEND 2) ADJECTIVE

sidekick, a pet ____________. They just barely beat the hot dog
BIRD

and ____________. Next, we will ____________ the prize for
FOOD VERB

Most Creative Costume. Our top vote-getters are the severed

____________ costume and everyone's favorite ____________-
BODY PART ADJECTIVE

haired artist, Bob Ross. It was very close, but the winner

is the world famous artist! Our final category, Sexiest

Costume, was the closest one tonight. There are so many

beautiful ____________ and ____________ hunks here tonight.
PLURAL NOUN ADJECTIVE

For the women, the top prize goes to the ____________
ADJECTIVE

____________! Let's have a round of applause! And now, it's time
OCCUPATION

for the gorgeous guys! The vote leaders were the ____________
ADJECTIVE

lumberjack and a(n) ____________ ____________ player. It was
ADJECTIVE SPORT

so close, we had to recount the votes ______ times! And it's the
NUMBER

lumberjack for the win!

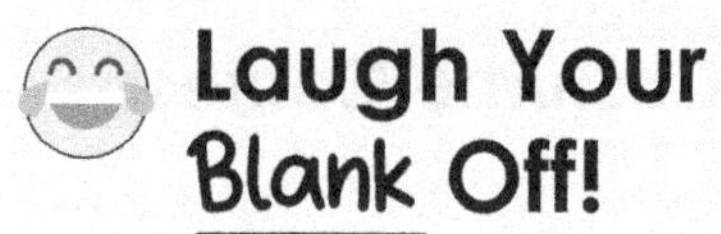

How to Carve a Jack-O'-Lantern

VERB
ADJECTIVE
ADJECTIVE
ADJECTIVE
PLURAL NOUN
NOUN
VERB
ADJECTIVE
ADJECTIVE
PLURAL NOUN
ADJECTIVE
PLURAL NOUN
ADJECTIVE
VERB ENDING IN "ING"
NOUN
ADJECTIVE
VERB
ADJECTIVE

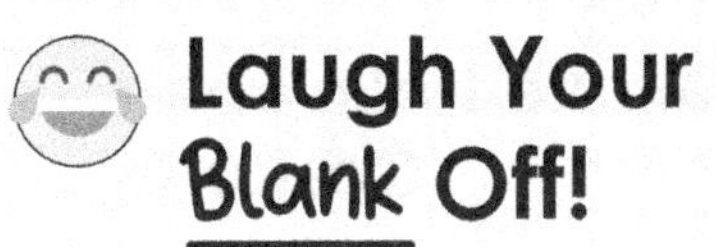

How to Carve a Jack-O'-Lantern

Halloween is almost here! That means it's time to ____________ (VERB) to the pumpkin patch and select a(n) ____________ (ADJECTIVE) carving pumpkin. Whether you're aiming for creepy or ____________ (ADJECTIVE), here are tips for creating the perfect jack-o'-lantern: 1) Make sure you pick a(n) ____________ (ADJECTIVE) pumpkin. You want to choose one that is free of ____________ (PLURAL NOUN) and has a flat ____________ (NOUN). You don't want it to ____________ (VERB) off the table when you cut into it. 2) Play some ____________ (ADJECTIVE) Halloween tunes for inspiration! 3) Cut a(n) ____________ (ADJECTIVE) top for your pumpkin and remove it. 4) Scoop out all of the ____________ (PLURAL NOUN). You can cook the seeds for a(n) ____________ (ADJECTIVE) treat. Make sure you thin out the ____________ (PLURAL NOUN) of the pumpkin a little, so you can carve it more easily. 5) Sketch a(n) ____________ (ADJECTIVE) design on your pumpkin. 6) Starting with the easiest lines of your design, begin ____________ (VERB ENDING IN "ING"). 7) Put a ____________ (NOUN)-powered candle inside to give your creation a(n) ____________ (ADJECTIVE) glow. 8) Put your jack-'o-lantern outside your door so everyone can ____________ (VERB) it! Repeat these steps as many times as you like to create a(n) ____________ (ADJECTIVE) collection of jack-'o-lanterns.

Last-Minute Halloween Costume

VERB
VERB
NOUN
ADJECTIVE
CLOTHING ITEM (PLURAL)
BODY PART
ADJECTIVE
CLOTHING ITEM
PLURAL NOUN
EXCLAMATION
ADJECTIVE
VERB
ADJECTIVE
NOUN
ADJECTIVE
ADJECTIVE
ADJECTIVE
BODY PART
PLURAL NOUN

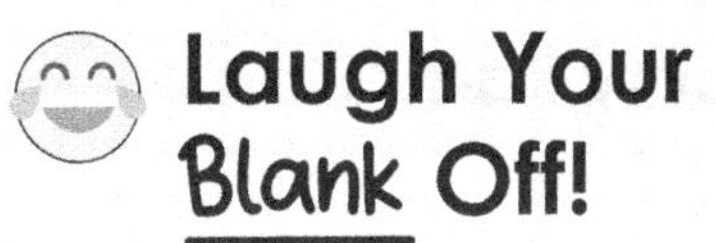

Last-Minute Halloween Costume

Have you left your Halloween costume until the last minute? At a loss for ideas of what to __________ (VERB)? Well, you don't have to __________ (VERB). __________ (NOUN) Magazine has you covered. If you are looking for something __________ (ADJECTIVE) and easy, throw on a pair of black __________ (CLOTHING ITEM (PLURAL)) and paint your __________ (BODY PART) white. Add a(n) __________ (ADJECTIVE) beret, __________ (CLOTHING ITEM), and a scarf. And presto! You're a mime. Perfect for __________ (PLURAL NOUN) who don't want to talk all night anyway! It's raining men, __________ (EXCLAMATION)! Grab a(n) __________ (ADJECTIVE) umbrella, some string, and a few magazines for this one. __________ (VERB) out photos of __________ (ADJECTIVE) men and hang them from the umbrella with the string. Slip on your __________ (NOUN) boots and you're good to go! Bonus points if you sing the song too, nice and __________ (ADJECTIVE)! Finally, try reliving your __________ (ADJECTIVE) years. Throw on some __________ (ADJECTIVE) sweatpants and sneakers, and grab a clipboard. Instant camp counselor! If you have a whistle to wear around your __________ (BODY PART), even better! Finding a Halloween costume can be tricky, but you have plenty of __________ (PLURAL NOUN) around your house to whip one up!

PLURAL NOUN
VERB ENDING IN "ING"
ADJECTIVE
NUMBER
NOUN
NOUN
ADJECTIVE
ALCOHOLIC SPIRIT
BEVERAGE
BEVERAGE
PLURAL NOUN
NOUN
NOUN
BODY PART
VERB
ADJECTIVE

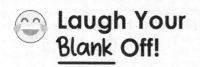

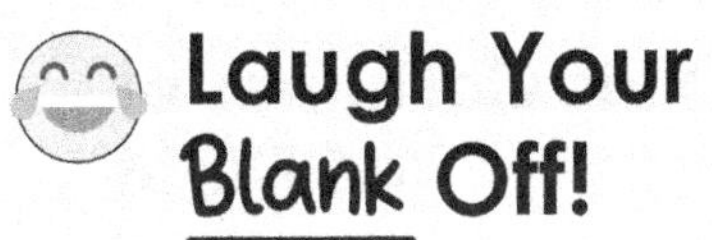

Scary Party Games

Halloween games are not just for ____________ (PLURAL NOUN), of course! If you're throwing a party this year, it's time to start ____________ (VERB ENDING IN "ING") about ____________ (ADJECTIVE) games to thrill your guests. Here are some winning ideas: 1) Murder Mystery – If you're having at least ____________ (NUMBER) guests, this is a great option. Everyone will become a ____________ (NOUN). Bonus points if they dress up to match! Then, you will work together to find the evil ____________ (NOUN). 2) Halloween Jinx - Come up with a list of ____________ (ADJECTIVE) words that will be declared "jinxed". If someone says one of the jinxed words, they have to drink a shot. It can be something strong, like ____________ (ALCOHOLIC SPIRIT), or just disgusting, like ____________ (BEVERAGE) mixed with ____________ (BEVERAGE). 3) Scary Hide-and-Seek – Turning off the ____________ (PLURAL NOUN) makes this game extra spooky. Beware of things that go bump in the ____________ (NOUN)! 4) Pass-It-On Ghost Story – It's nice to play this game by ____________ (NOUN)-light. One person whispers a few sentences from a spooky tale in the ____________ (BODY PART) of the person next to them. That person repeats the story to the next person, and so on. The last person ____________ (VERB) the story out loud. But by that point, it's a twisted tale indeed! So ____________ (ADJECTIVE)!

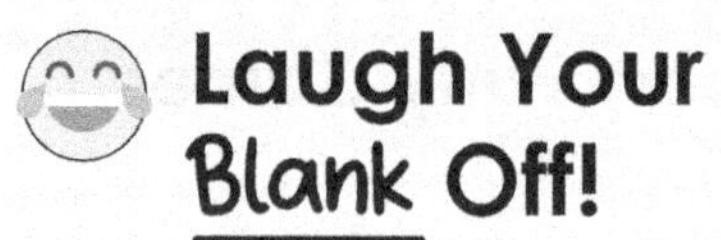

Best Kids Costumes of the NIght

PLURAL NOUN
ADJECTIVE
BODY PART
VERB (PAST TENSE)
FIRST NAME (ANYONE)
CLOTHING ITEM
COLOR
NOUN
SILLY NOISE
NUMBER
NUMBER
PLURAL NOUN
PLURAL NOUN
PLURAL NOUN
ANIMAL (PLURAL)
PLURAL NOUN
NOUN
VERB ENDING IN "ING"
NOUN

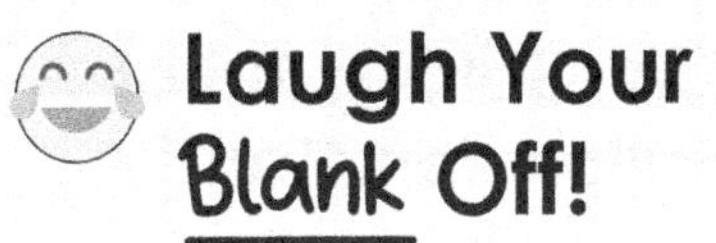

Best Kids Costumes of the NIght

Now that I'm forced to be an adult, I miss racing from house to house on Halloween collecting candy. Chewy ____________ (PLURAL NOUN) were my favorite! But getting to see the ____________ (ADJECTIVE) costumes kids are wearing when they come to my door, puts a big smile on my ____________ (BODY PART). This year, a tiny Batman ____________ (VERB (PAST TENSE)) onto my porch. "Where's your sidekick, ____________ (FIRST NAME (ANYONE))?" I asked. Then I spotted his masked Dad on the sidewalk, wearing a flowing ____________ (CLOTHING ITEM) and ____________ (COLOR) tights! Two of my neighbors dressed up as my favorite characters from ____________ (NOUN) *Story*: ____________ (SILLY NOISE) Lightyear and Woody. I saw ____________ (NUMBER) princesses, ____________ (NUMBER) vampires, five ____________ (PLURAL NOUN) and several "celebrities." Would you believe that the Backstreet ____________ (PLURAL NOUN) and the Spice ____________ (PLURAL NOUN) actually came to my house?! The cats and ____________ (ANIMAL (PLURAL)) and furry ____________ (PLURAL NOUN) were as adorable as ever. But it's hard to top ____________ (NOUN)-breathing dragons. Especially when it's a whole family, including a Baby Dragon, just ____________ (VERB ENDING IN "ING") out of her eggshell. Of course, I would still love to go trick-or-treating myself. Maybe I could pass myself off as a really big ____________ (NOUN)?

Tips for Getting Rid of Halloween Candy

COLOR
VERB ENDING IN “ING”
NUMBER
NOUN
ADJECTIVE
ADJECTIVE
ADJECTIVE
NOUN
VERB
ADJECTIVE
NOUN
ADJECTIVE
VERB
VERB
VERB ENDING IN “ING”
ADJECTIVE

Tips for Getting Rid of Halloween Candy

Did you and your kids eat so much Halloween candy that you're turning ____________ COLOR? Are you looking for a good way to get rid of candy without ____________ VERB ENDING IN "ING" it all yourself? Don't worry, you can save some treats for later. ____________ NUMBER pieces is probably enough, right? For extra candy, try these tips: 1) Donate it to your local food ____________ NOUN. Candy is not a(n) ____________ ADJECTIVE food, but everyone likes a(n) ____________ ADJECTIVE treat now and then. 2) Have a Swap Meet with your kids. In exchange for their candy, give them things like ____________ ADJECTIVE stickers, more ____________ NOUN time, or money. Everyone ____________ VERB money, right? 3) Treats for Troops. This ____________ ADJECTIVE program collects candy and sends it to service members all over the ____________ NOUN. What a cool way to say "Thank you!" And guess, what? The ____________ ADJECTIVE candy collection site is probably your dentist's office! 4) "Take Your Candy to Work Day" - Some of your coworkers will ____________ VERB you for it and some will ____________ VERB you! Don't worry! You won't be the only one ____________ VERB ENDING IN "ING" extra candy to work. Hey, maybe the boss would swap candy for cash. Talk about a(n) ____________ ADJECTIVE deal!

Thank you for trying us out

A favor please 

Would you take a quick minute to leave us a rating/review on Amazon? It makes a *HUGE* difference and we would really appreciate it!

More fun from JBC Story Press

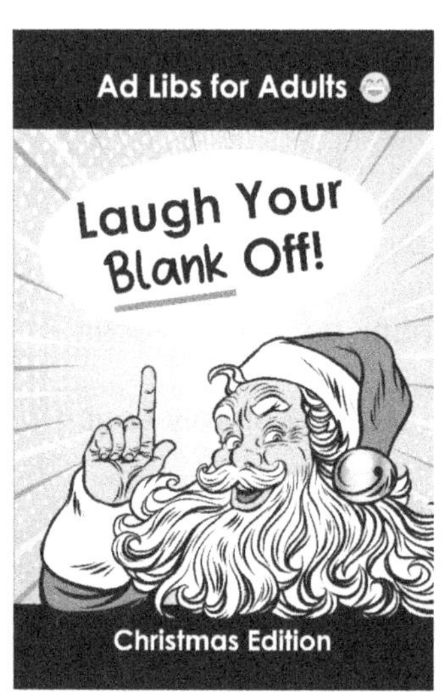

To see more, visit this link **http://amazon.com/author/jbcstory** or scan this code!

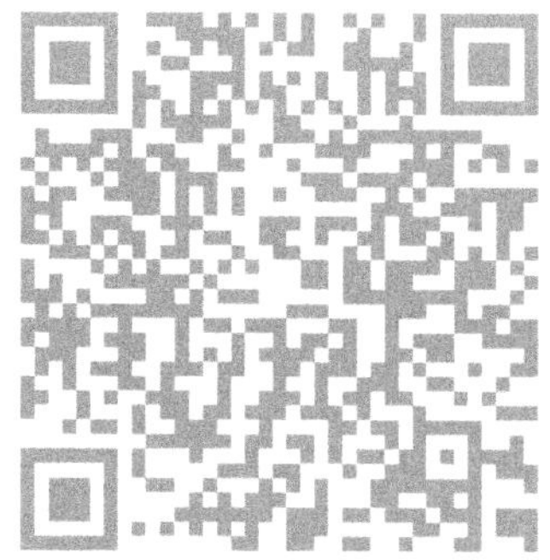

Do you like freebies?
Please send email to
info@jbcempowerpress.com
and we'll send you free funny stuff!

Made in United States
Orlando, FL
24 September 2023

37239854R00026